MW01295171

Although the Author and Editor have made every effort to ensure that the information in this book was correct at press time, the author does not assume and hereby disclaim any liability to any party for any loss, damage, or disruption caused by errors or omissions, whether such errors or omissions result from negligence, accident, or any other cause.

Foreword

This interesting book that is before you should be considered as an effort of the very few trained urologists in Zambia that have devoted their lives to this extremely interesting and exciting field of medicine that is still by far underdeveloped in the region. One of the main problems that is facing Urology in the developing world is the lack of general information pertaining to what urology is really about and it is not unusual that many students during their education at medical school are under exposed to this field.

There is also a general misperception that urological focus is mainly on the elderly male population; this could not be further from the truth as this only represents one segment of urological practice and not even major one in an environment like ours where the majority of the population is young (below 18 years of age).

This book is written in a simple language that is easily understandable to a final year medical student as well as young doctors who have just opened the doors of clinical practice. It is also meant for our future colleagues who are just joining the exciting world of Urology. They will all find enough of up to date information regarding the most common urological conditions and their treatment modalities. This book can also be a useful source for quick orientation and revision.

I firmly believe that this book should also be used as an invitation to all future Zambian and African urologists to join in and give their contribution to Urological development throughout this continent.

Dr. Nenad Spasojevic

Consultant Urologist

Acknowledgments

Several people unknowingly have had an impact on me throughout the course of compilation of this book. Special thanks go out to the entire urological fraternity here in Zambia without whom I would not have reached the heights I have. My sincere gratitude also goes to the following, without whom, the completion of this work would not have been possible:

❖   Dr Robert Zulu, Consultant General surgeon for the editorial commentary and invaluable direction, advice and support.

❖   Dr Bruce Bvulani, for the tremendous contributions to the pediatric urology section.

❖   Dr Simba Kaja, My husband for being a listening ear, a constant source of encouragement and inspiration

❖   Last but not least Mr Mwansa P. Chalwe my father, my ultimate mentor, sounding board and friend.

Dedication

This work is especially dedicated to a young man, Mwansa Chileya Chalwe Jnr. , who was wise beyond his years, though no longer with us, his values of excellence and humility will continue to inspire me and generations to come.

Table of Contents

General urology

Clinical skills

Abbreviations

a.	Artery
AD	Autonomic dysreflexia
AUR	Acute Urinary Retention
ATLS	Advanced Trauma Life support
AKI	Acute Kidney Injury
BPH	Benign Prostate Hypertrophy
Ca	Carcinoma
CT	Computed Tomography
DRE	Digital Rectal Examination
Fr	French gauge
GU	Genito-urinary
ICU	Intensive Care Unit
IV	Intravenous
IVF	Intravenous fluids
LUTS	Lower Urinary Tract Symptoms
mm.	Muscle
n.	Nerve
OPD	Out Patient Department
POD	Post Obstructive Diuresis
PSA	Prostate Specific Antigen
PUV	Posterior Urethral Valves
TURP	Transurethral resection of Prostate
TWOC	Trial Without Catheter
U/S	Ultrasound scan
v.	vein
Vs	Versus

Introduction

Beginners guide to UROLOGY provides a quick glance at practical urology for those with limited clinical exposure to this sub-specialty. These may include final year medical students and medical interns in surgical rotations. It can also be used as an adjunct for the trainee who has just commenced their surgical training and has no prior urology experience. It contains several scenarios that are common in day to day clinical practice in the surgical department. The booklet also provides an introduction to the most common urological aspects of surgery, and can act as a basis for a much broader and in depth understanding of more complex aspects of general urology.

The text is arranged in three distinct sections: *the body* which contains the main concepts of the topic, while the *side bars* contain a skill and tips on how to carry out the aforementioned skill. The exact technique for performing is not outlined in a step by step manner; however the principles surrounding the technique are emphasised in a way that will ensure that the reader can perform the said tasks with ease. Finally, at the conclusion of each topic a *note* is made of danger points or common errors to watch out for.

Beginners guide to UROLOGY is a collection of the basic skills and materials designed specifically as an aide to guide a student and provide a general overview at the field of urology. For students who may have had a relatively limited exposure to Urology as a surgical subspecialty, **Beginners guide to UROLOGY** is a simplified and concise tool for quick access to this exciting field. The overarching aim of this text is to provide an overview of the basic urological concepts specifically for students and trainees in resource limited settings.

Urethral Injury

Catheterisation is a common procedure performed on a daily basis in clinical practice. Iatrogenic urethral injury is a frequent occurrence that can be avoided by following a few basic principles. The consequences of urethral injury are far reaching, thus it is vital to avoid it at all costs.

Basic anatomy: The male urethra is divided into the anterior and posterior urethra divided by the urogenital diaphragm.

o   ***Anterior urethra;*** meatus, fossa navicularis, penile (pendulous urethra), bulbar urethra

o   ***Posterior urethra;*** membranous urethra, prostatic urethra

The blood supply to the urethra is very rich and arises from two main sources:

- o Bulbar arteries
- o Dorsal penile a.

Clinical scenarios

These are instances that would entail access to the urethra; care must be taken not to injure the urethra in any way in these instances.

1.   Elective surgery: some elective cases may require routine catheterisation in the pre op and post op period.

2.   Relief of bladder outlet obstruction: this is a common emergency room situation that would require urethral catheterisation.

3.   Urological interventions: endoscopic

4.   urologic procedures would require trans- urethral access.

Urethral bleeding
Urethral bleeding can be profuse and alarming due to the urethral rich blood supply.
Approach: weighted *perineal* compression initially for 3 minutes (which can be continued if bleeding persists) usually suffices. If bleeding is due to trauma urinary diversion in the form of a supra pubic cystostomy is indicated.

Urethral Catheterisation

The most basic urological skill, done correctly it should be:

- Atraumatic
- Aseptic
- Smooth
- Painless

Basic principles:

1.   Use the smallest possible sized catheter for the intended purpose. As a general rule; males can safely be catheterised using a size 14-16fr for simple bladder drainage. Females can safely be catheterised with a size 12-14fr catheter for simple bladder drainage.

2.   Preparation is vital; always arrange the necessary tools for the task prior to beginning. From the correct sized catheter, water for balloon inflation (if using a Foleys catheter), to lubrication, cleaning solutions and gloves. (see chapter on catheterisation)

3.   Insure adequate lubrication with Intraurethral lubricant to ensure smooth and safe passage of the catheter.

4.   If in doubt about position of the catheter in bladder, **DO NOT** inflate the balloon. Remove the catheter , try once again or ask for help!

5. Use distilled water (water for injection) to inflate the balloon

Suprapubic Cystostomy- SPC

This seemingly "trivial" procedure is the mainstay of treatment in several emergency situations more so in the case of a failed urethral catheterisation with a grossly distended bladder.

Basic anatomy:

The basic landmark for a suprapubic cystostomy is 2cm above the pubic symphysis. *!!!!Remember: mark, aspirate, cut, aspirate- always be sure you are directly above the bladder as you perform an SPC!!!!*

Layers of the anterior abdominal wall up to the bladder:

o   skin
o   camper's fascia
o   scarpa's fascia
o   anterior leaf of rectus sheath (at this level the posterior leaf is deficient)
o   rectus abdominis muscle
o   perivesical fat
o   bladder

Clinical scenarios

These are instances that would require you to perform an SPC.
1.   Acute urinary retention with failed urethral catheterisation
2.   Urethral trauma (iatrogenic or external trauma)
3.   Urinary diversion on the background of extensive perineal injury/damage e.g. Fournier's gangrene, other ulcerative lesions, trauma.

Failed catheterisation
Sometimes urethral catheterisation fails, a few manoeuvres can be attempted prior to SPC insertion.
•   Adequate lubrication of urethra (Squeeze 10 CC SYRINGE filled with lubricant into the urethra) and re attempt urethral catheterisation.
•   Perform a suprapubic puncture with a wide bore canula, to partially empty the bladder then re attempt urethral catheter insertion.

The retained catheter

In the advent that you come across a catheter that just will not come out remember:

1.   As long as the catheter is draining, a retained catheter is not an emergency
2.   **DO NOT** attempt to over inflate and burst the balloon
3.   **AVOID** manoeuvres that may end with the catheter retracting all the way back into the bladder: a simple procedure will now become open surgery!

Options for removal:

Ensure the catheter is still draining!

▪   Cut the valve and allow the balloon to drain spontaneously- this requires patience!
▪   A stylet through the balloon channel will unblock the channel and can be used to safely deflate the balloon without rupture.
▪   Trans abdominal Ultrasound guided piercing (PUNCTURE) of the balloon with a canula will safely deflate the balloon
▪   When in doubt STOP and ask for HELP

In some cases endoscopic removal may be warranted- this is done by the urologist.

NOTE: SPC is ABSOLUTELY contraindicated in cases of bladder cancer or if there is suspicion of bladder cancer

Post Obstructive Diuresis

After relief of Acute Urinary Retention, it is vital to look out for post obstructive diuresis, such patients should be observed overnight to ensure this relatively rare complication of complete bladder outlet obstruction is not missed.

Basic concepts

Once obstruction is released, the kidneys respond by increasing urine production leading to polyuria. This response is usually self limiting however if it proceeds beyond 72hours can have significant consequences ranging from dehydration, electrolyte imbalance and even renal failure.

As a general rule, a diuresis of more than 200ml/hr for more than 12hours is enough to make the diagnosis.

Approach to the obstructed patient

1.   Relief of AUR is vital, in the case of obstructive uropathy, this alone can resolve derangements of renal function
2.   Once obstruction is overcome, oral fluid intake should be encouraged.
3.   The azotemic patient should be treated with careful IVF administration while on continuous catheter drainage
4.   Catheters should never be clamped until renal function is established

---

Management of POD
*   Hypotonic 0.45% saline at a rate of half the urine output at 2hourly intervals
*   Strict monitoring of input and output
*   Urine specific gravity can be used both to determine the nature of POD and to monitor for its resolution

---

Acute Urinary Retention (AUR)

This is the single most common urological presentation to the emergency room. It should be born in mind that this is not only a urological emergency but a *surgical* emergency. Prompt relief is the only treatment option.

NOTE:

1.   LUBRICATION IS KEY! A sufficiently lubricated catheter should pass into the bladder with minimal resistance.
2.   Younger adult males can also present with BOO secondary to prostatic causes (prostatitis) catheterisation should be uneventful in these cases.
3.   Females can also present in AUR, catheterisation is usually uneventful.
4.   In children, constipation may cause voiding dysfunction including AUR.
5.   Post operative patients following surgery in the perineum such as haemorrhoidectomy and male circumcision. Usually due to inadequate pain control
6.   In cases with no obvious cause of retention think of *neurogenic* causes, do a spinal exam, a full neurologic exam and beware of *autonomic dysreflexia*

Finally, after relief of retention observe patients for *Post Obstructive Diuresis (see later section)*

Bladder trauma

The bladder is one of the commonly injured genitourinary organs in adults. Injury is usually secondary to blunt force trauma and most patients are polytrauma cases. Approximately 60-80% of pelvic fractures will have concomitant bladder injury while approximately 20% of bladder injuries will have concomitant pelvic injury. The injuries are predominantly extra peritoneal and can usually be managed conservatively.

Basic anatomy:

The bladder is normally a pelvic organ except when distended. It is an extra peritoneal organ and **does not** communicate with the abdominal cavity.

Assessment of suspected bladder injury
o   The standard ATLS principles apply- remember this is a trauma patient.
o   Focused urological exam should include a digital rectal exam
o   Failure to void with signs of peritonism are almost always indicative of an intra peritoneal rupture- indication for *2 layer vesicorraphy* with absorbable sutures

Remember; the decision on surgical Vs conservative management may have to be made clinically in case of absence of imaging modalities in the emergency setting.

Clinical scenarios: These are instances that should raise your index of suspicion for bladder injury.

1.   Stable patient with no other symptoms apart from failure to void, following blunt force abdominal trauma with no features of acute urinary retention. *(intraperitoneal)*

2.   Otherwise stable patient with sudden onset hematuria, suprapubic bruising and a history of blunt force trauma to the lower abdomen. *(extraperitoneal)*

The gold standard diagnostic test for bladder injury remains a cystogram on a fully distended bladder.

Catheterisation and bladder trauma
This is a safe procedure in cases of bladder trauma. A "dry" catheterisation is almost always diagnostic for intra peritoneal bladder injury. While bloody urine suggests the bladder is intact or the injury is a small and extra peritoneal one. Catheters being used for conservative management should be left in situ on *CONTINOUS DRAINAGE for* a minimum of 14days.

Imaging modalities in bladder trauma

Cystography

This contrast study is the gold standard diagnostic test for all suspected bladder injuries.

1.   Active filling using a bladder syringe is preferred over passive bladder filling.
2.   The bladder must be filled with more than 400mls in order to identify extravasation
3.   Both AP and lateral views must be taken
4.   "flame-like" appearance of contrast on AP views is indicative of extra peritoneal bladder injury

Plain x-ray

Is useful in identification of concomitant skeletal injuries (pelvic fractures, rib fractures) it is however not routinely used to diagnose bladder trauma.

Abdominal U/S

Abdominal U/S cannot be used to make a definitive diagnosis of bladder injury. Rather, It is typically used to perform the "FAST scan"- Focused Assesment with Sonography for Trauma.

Renal trauma

The kidneys are the most commonly injured genitourinary organ. Most injury is secondary to blunt force trauma and in most cases can be managed conservatively, however, if un-recognised, renal trauma, can be life threatening.

Basic concepts:

Kidneys are retroperitoneal organs and are usually well protected from injury, certain circumstances predispose kidneys to injury even from seemingly trivial force:

1. *Young children*
2. *Hydronephrotic kidneys*
3. *Ectopic kidneys esp. pelvic kidneys*

Layers of the lateral abdominal wall/ flank:

o   Skin
o   External oblique mm.
o   Internal oblique mm.
o   Tranversus abdominis mm.
o   Transversalis fascia
o   Peritoneum

Approach to renal trauma

1. The basic ATLS principles apply; remember the A, B, C s- this is a trauma patient!
2. Frequent monitoring of vitals(especially BP, Pulse) is key
3. Contrast enhanced CT scan is the gold standard for diagnosis and grading of injury
4. In the case of a pulsatile, expanding retroperitoneal hematoma (during exploratory laparotomy) a trauma nephrectomy may be indicated even without prior diagnostic imaging.
5. The hemodynamically stable, *responders* may be managed conservatively, with close monitoring; however be prepared to intervene if hemodynamic status changes.

Hematuria in renal trauma
Hematuria is not a reliable indicator of the extent of renal trauma. Hematuria maybe absent even in the face of high grade renal trauma. Despite this, dipstick urinanalysis is a good tool for *follow up* of the renal trauma.

Conservative management of renal trauma

❖   Strict bed rest and avoidance of strenuous activity
❖   Serial dipstick urinanalysis to monitor for resolution of hematuria

Removal of urinary catheter

In patients who may have been catheterised for more than 14days bladder training maybe required

❖   Spigot the catheter a few days prior to planned removal
❖   Gradually increase intervals between bladder emptying to improve irritative symptoms

Fournier's gangrene

The single most feared urological emergency, Fournier's gangrene is a fulminant, necrotising fasciitis of the perineum, scrotum and penis that carries a high mortality rate. On initial presentation the patients may be deceptively "stable" thus a high index of suspicion for all cases of peno-scrotal inflammation or swelling is required. Once suspected no time should be wasted on diagnosis- this is a surgical emergency!!!*Remember: "over diagnosis" of Fournier's gangrene is better than a missed diagnosis of Fournier's gangrene.*

Basic anatomy The fascial planes of the anterior abdomen are contagious with the fascia of the genital and perineum.

o   Skin
o   Camper's fatty layer
o   Scarpa's fascia→ Bucks fascia of penis→Dartos of scrotum→ Colles fascia of perineum
*Note: Scarpa's fascia extends anteriorly to the clavicles thus infection can extend along this plane (Melleney's gangrene)
The testicles are usually spared as their blood supply is from the *testicular a.* a direct branch of the Aorta thus orchidectomy is rarely required.

Approach to Fournier's gangrene
1.   High index of suspicion; even slight scrotal edema with seemingly normal overlying skin, in susceptible patients should be considered Fournier's gangrene until ruled out!
2.   IV access with 2 large bore canulas
3.   Fluid resuscitation
4.   Broad spectrum IV antibiotics (penicillins + aminogylcosides + nitroimidazoles or 3rd gen. cephalosporins+ quinolones+ nitroimidazoles)
5.   Immediate SURGICAL DEBRIDEMENT; wide, extensive debridement of ALL necrotic tissues until healthy boarders are reached
6.   Serial 2nd, 3rd and even 4th look debridement as necess.
7.   AGRESSIVENESS is the mainstay of treatment

> RED LIGHT!!!!
> Any patient with a history of difficulty voiding that presents with a peno-scrotal swelling should be accessed for urine extravasation as they could be an impending Fournier's gangrene.

Urosepsis

Recognition of the condition is paramount to adequate management.

1.   Thorough history and examination, focused urological exam including a digital rectal examination

Take note of the consistency of the prostate; beware of a prostatic abscess

2.   IV access with wide bore canula and Fluid resuscitation
3.   Combination broad spectrum antibiotics with adequate urine penetration(e.g. quinolones, aminoglycocides)
4.   Urethral catheterisation: provide drainage of infected urine on the background of bladder outlet obstruction. Secondarily for Input and Output monitoring

Elderly patients that are apathic, hypothermic, and hypotensive with LUTS or a history of LUTS should raise suspicion of urosepsis

Scrotal swelling

This is a considerably common presentation both to the emergency and outpatient departments. The acute scrotum is both a surgical as well as urological emergency as it may represent conditions requiring urgent surgical intervention.

Basic concepts:

Scrotal layers	Scrotal content
Skin	Spermatic cord
Dartos fascia	Testes
External spermatic fascia	Epidydmis
Cremasteric fascia	
Internal spermatic fascia	
Tunica vaginalis	

An understanding of the scrotal content will lead to a clearer and easier differential diagnostic process

Approach to scrotal swelling

1.   Always carry out a *full clinical examination*, including a focused urological examination complete with a digital rectal exam rather than an isolated genital examination.

2.   Always have **Fournier's gangrene** as a differential if scrotal swelling presents with crepitus, and systemic or constitutional signs and symptoms.

3.   An incarcerated hernia may present like a testicular torsion.

4.   An acute scrotal swelling on the background of LUTS must raise suspicion for urinary extravasation and/ or urinoma formation

5.   Avoid aspiration of scrotal swellings **suspected** to be hydroceles, use other modalities (transillumination test, scrotal U/S) to confirm diagnosis

Testicular Torsion

This is a true surgical emergency; precious time should not be wasted on diagnostic imaging. The decision for scrotal exploration should be made promptly as testicular salvage is directly related to time from onset of symptoms.

1.   Scrotal exploration should be done within the shortest possible time from patient presentation

2.   Patients need to be counselled and consent for possible *orchidectomy*

3.   Bilateral orchidopexy , with non absorbable sutures is absolutely indicated in the case of testicular torsion, never do a unilateral orchidopexy

4.   Orchidectomy of the non viable testes with contralateral orchidopexy is standard practice

---

Scrotal imaging

The age of a patient with a scrotal swelling is a vital tool in formulating the differential diagnosis. Generally older men present with more benign causes while in the younger age population scrotal swellings can be ominous signs requiring further investigation and diagnostic work up. Scrotal U/S is safe and readily accessible imaging modality with a high sensitivity profile.

Testicular mass

Testicular masses are not a common presentation; testicular malignancy generally represents 1% of all urological malignancy, however all testicular masses should be adequately investigated.

Basic concepts

Structure of testes

Caput epididymis→efferent ductules→rete testes→straight tubules→seminiferous tubules

These are encased in the tunica albugenia and the bi- layered tunica vaginalis

Tumours of the testes

Broadly these can be classified as

- Germ cell (seminoma and non seminoma)
- Stromal (leydig, sertoli cell)
- Others: secondary tumours, lymphomas, paratesticular tumours

Most tumours are mixed and have components of some or all of the histological subtypes

Approach to testicular masses

1. A complete history to illicit possible risk factors as well as a full physical examination
2. A focused urological examination taking note of any palpable retroperitoneal masses

Note: the consistency of the mass solid vs. cystic, painful vs. painless.

3. Serum tumour markers must be taken before the decision for orchidectomy is made
4. In general a hard painless mass in a young patient is considered malignant until proven otherwise.

Management of testicular tumours
Cases of TB orchitis may be difficult to clinically differentiate from testicular malignancy even on scrotal U/S; orchidectomy remains the mainstay of diagnosis. Testicular tumours generally respond well to currently available treatment modalities.

High inguinal orchidectomy

In the case of a suspicious testicular mass, imaging via a scrotal U/S is highly sensitive.

Diagnostic algorithm testicular mass

1. Scrotal U/S
2. Serum tumour markers (AFP, LDH Bhcg)

Staging modalities include:

1. Chest x-ray
2. Abdominal CT
3. Brain CT (if symptomatic)

Principles of the high inguinal orchidectomy

1. Access via an inguinal incision
2. Early cord control
3. High ligation at the internal inguinal ring
4. Delivery of testes into incision

Incision can be extended to the scrotum once cord control has been attained if the tumour is too bulky.

5. Complete the orchidectomy

Priapism

This is a urological emergency and treatment is aimed at prompt decompression to avoid irreversible corporal fibrosis.

In managing a case of priapism, always counsel patients on the possibility of loss of erectile function that may ensue even after deflation. It is directly correlated to the length of time of penile tumescence.

Approach to priapism

1.   Analgesia, hydration and sedation are the initial steps.
2.   Corporal aspiration and irrigation with saline till bright red blood is aspirated
3.   Vasoactive agents can be used if aspiration alone fails. 1ml aliquots of phenylephrine over a 20min period should lead to detumescence

These agents should only be given under strict cardiac monitoring!!!

4.   If above measures fail, a urological / senior consult is warranted. STOP ,CALL FOR HELP
5.   Shunting procedures are best in the hands of one who is sufficiently familiar with the relevant anatomy to avoid subsequent complications
6.   After 24hrs the salvage rate is almost zero and such patients would be candidates for immediate penile prosthesis.

Late presentation of Priapism

if priapism has lasted >72hrs the chances of preserved erectile function are minimal, management is aimed at adequate analgesia and hydration.
Shunting procedures should not be attempted in these cases as cavernosal fibrosis would have already set in.

Paraphimosis

A common presentation in various age groups. This is a urological emergency.

Once identified can be managed effectively with few sequelae

Features;

• Non retractile prepuce
• Constrictive ring
• Fissures
• Edema below the ring
• Desiccation of exposed glans

The simplest way to reduce a paraphimosis is via gentle sustained pressure of the oedematous prepuce for 3 minutes, followed by gentle traction while simultaneously pushing down on the glans penis.

Note:

An elective circumcision may be offered to the patient at a later stage.

Remember: avoid piercing of the skin in attempts to reduce the edema due to the high risk of infection.

Hematuria

The single most ominous urological sign is hematuria. As a general rule *"hematuria is a urological malignancy until proven otherwise"*. All patients presenting with hematuria must undergo a **hematuria work up.**

Basic concepts

Hematuria can be;

- **visible or non visible i.e. macro Vs microscopic**
- **Initial, total or terminal**
- **painless or painful**

For women especially those of reproductive age, presenting with hematuria remember to take a gynaecological history including a history of last menses, some gynaecological conditions and emergencies can inadvertently end up in a surgical ward!!

Approach to hematuria An understanding of the possible sources of hematuria is vital

Upper tract:

- Renal – nephrological Vs urological (casts with proteinuria on the urinanalysis indicates a likely Nephrological cause)
Urological: renal stones, Renal Cell Carcinoma, Transitional Cell Carcinoma
- Ureteric- stones, Transitional Cell Carcinoma, blood clot

Lower tract:
- Ureteric: **transitional cell carcinoma**, stones
- Bladder: **malignancy**, stones, infections
- Prostatic: BPH, **Ca prostate**
- Urethral bleeding: strictures, urethritis, stone

The hematuria work up

Each of the possible sources of hematuria must be evaluated in order to direct further urological assessment.

1. Urinanalysis
2. Abdominal ultrasound scan
3. Plain abdominal pelvic x-ray commonly called K.U.B
4. Urethrocystoscopy
5. Focused urological assessment then follows based on the above findings

All hematuria or history of hematuria should be documented and followed up. Even transient hematuria MUST be investigated.

Post operative hematuria
Post operative hematuria can be expected in most urological surgery. It is most common in prostate and bladder surgery:
Examples:
- Prostatectomy (open or trans urethral)
- Trans Urethral Resection of bladder tumors
- Ureteric re-implantation
- Cystolithotomy
This hematuria is usually self limiting and no further investigation is indicated.

Orchitis

Acute orchitis can present as an acute scrotum with a very distressed patient. There are various causes of orchitis however the principles of management remain the same.

Basic concepts

Orchitis is usually secondary to retrograde flow of infection from a primary genito-urinary site.
Infection can travel from the bladder to the prostate, through the ejaculatory ducts into the seminal vesicles, via the vas to the epididymis and ultimately the testes.
Orchitis can be;

- Bacterial
- Viral
- Tuberculous
- Xanthomatous (rare)

Approach to orchitis

1. General examination with focused urological examination including a digital rectal exam

Note: always examine the spermatic cord and epididymis bilaterally

2. The Cremasteric reflex and the Prehn's test may be difficult to illicit in an acutely inflamed testes that is adherent to the overlying skin.
3. The acutely inflamed testes usually has the normal lie in the scrotum and the patient may have overt signs of an inflammatory reaction, adequate history and examination can usually aid in the differential diagnosis.
4. Treatment is **2-week** course of antibiotics and anti inflammatory drugs with scrotal support and rest

---

Testicular torsion Vs Orchitis

In some cases the distinction between these two entities is difficult to make. The general rule applies: "a negative scrotal exploration is better than a missed testicular torsion"- if in doubt do a scrotal exploration. Overall teenagers and young adults present with torsion while in the elderly, usually with LUTS, orchitis is more the rule than the exception

Prostatitis

In younger adult males presenting with AUR with constitutional symptoms acute prostatitis should be among the top differentials.

The digital rectal exam reveals an exquisitely tender prostate

1. Relief of retention is vital and the catheter should be kept on continuous irrigation
2. alpha-blockers should be continued until catheter removal
3. Prostate penetrative antibiotic therapy should continue for 14-21 days
4. NSAIDs are vital to reduce inflammation, which contributes to the bladder outlet obstruction

Note: an acutely inflamed prostate feels soft Vs a prostatic abscess that is characteristically boggy

Prostatic abscess

This is usually a clinical diagnosis; Trans rectal U/S guided drainage with adequate IV antibiotic cover is advised.

Renal colic

A renal colic is a term that broadly refers to any presentation of pain that is thought to arise from conditions affecting the kidney. Renal colic can present with exquisite pain that is characteristically located in the flank and may be described as irradiating to the groin and lower back.

Basic anatomy

Renal blood supply:

Renal artery→posterior + anterior branches→segmental branches→interlobar branches→ arcuate arteries→interlobular branches

Note: Renal arteries are end arteries!!

Collecting system:

Nephron→ collecting duct→papillary duct (of renal pyramid) →minor calyx→major calyx→renal pelvis→ureter

The pain of renal colic is generally caused by distension of the renal capsule, which can be due to:

- Hydronephrosis (Dietl's crisis)
- Infections(pyelonephritis)
- Pyonephrosis
- Obstructing/ impacted ureteric stone

Small renal stones, and stones passed into the bladder usually do not cause renal colic and may be asymptomatic.

Approach to renal colic

1.   The patient with renal colic typically is agitated and anxious, and is usually pacing or wriggling in pain.
2.   A full physical examination including a focused urological examination will reveal marked costal vertebral angle tenderness with an unremarkable abdominal examination
3.   These patients are frequently dehydrated, due to the vomiting and nausea that often accompanies a renal colic
4.   **Symptom relief** is the main treatment goal in the acute setting. Definitive urological management follows after resolution of the acute episode

Management of Renal colic

Symptom relief is the main treatment goal. Definitive management (e.g. stone removal, stenting, ureteric re-implantation) are carried out upon resolution of acute episode.

1.   Adequate analgesia ranging from NSAIDS, opiods and narcotic analgesics
2.   Hydration
3.   Anti emetics
4.   Appropriate IV antibiotic cover

Note: opiods and narcotic analgesics either orally or by intravenous route are both safe and appropriate in the management of renal colic.

Scrotal trauma

Scrotal trauma can present as part of a polytrauma case or as an isolated injury.
The severity of injury ranges from bruises, to lacerations and degloving wounds or complete avulsion.

Basic anatomy
Spermatic cord contents: (the rule of 3s)

3 arteries;
Testicular, deferential, cremasteric
3 nerves;
Genital branch of genitor-femoral n., cremasteric n., sympathetic nerve fibres, (ilio-inguinal n. is **on** not **in** the cord)
3 others;
Vas deferens, pampiniform plexus, lymphatic's

Approach to scrotal trauma
1.   Basic ATLS principles- this is a trauma patient!
2.   After a general examination, a focused urological exam should include a digital rectal exam.
Note: Scrotal trauma may include perineal and rectal injuries.
3.   Adequate debridement of non viable tissues and suturing is adequate in many cases; wider lacerations with scrotal loss may require a graft in an elective setting.
4.   Ensure integrity of scrotal contents as these can be a source of troublesome bleeding
5.   Scrotal elevation is a vital step in the management of these injuries to avoid edema which can impair wound healing

---

Danger points!
In some instances, scrotal trauma maybe secondary to a bite (human or animal), **DONOT** suture such injuries. In such cases the risk of Fournier's gangrene is very high and adequate debridement, and IV antibiotics therapy is warranted. A delayed approach to repair is acceptable.

Testicular injury

Testicular injury usually presents in combination with scrotal trauma.

Scrotal edema can be alarmingly large and in the setting of substantial blunt force trauma, a high index of suspicion for testicular injury is required

1.   Ecchymosis, and increasing scrotal swelling indicate ongoing bleeding
2.   Testicular rupture is difficult to diagnose clinically ,scrotal U/S is diagnostic
3.   Scrotal exploration with repair of the defect in the T. albugenia is recommended
4.   Stable scrotal swelling can be managed conservatively with elevation , anti-inflammatory drugs and antibiotics

Penile trauma

Isolated penile trauma is rare, and the most common presentation of penile injury involve cases with force aimed directly to the penis.

Basic anatomy

Layers of the penis;

- Skin
- Dartos fascia
- Areolar tissue
- Bucks fascia
- Tunica albuginea (bilaminar)

Vessels and nerves running through the layers; Superficial dorsal penile v., Deep dorsal penile v., Dorsal penile arteries

Types of injury

1. Blunt force
2. Penetrating
a. Lacerations
b. Stab wounds
c. Human bites
3. Degloving wound
4. Amputation –partial/ complete

Approach to penile trauma

Penile trauma can be an alarming presentation with a visibly large amount bleeding in proportion to the site of injury.

- The basic principles of managing a trauma patient apply.
- Adequate debridement and suturing should be done

Note: if there is suspicion of urethral trauma CALL the urologist.

Penile amputation: macro-vascular repair and repair of dorsal penile nerve together with urethral re-anastomosis is usually sufficient to repair a total penile amputation

---

Antibiotic cover in penile trauma

Genital injuries have the potential for developing Fournier's gangrene and as such adequate antibiotic cover should always be part of management of such injuries. Judicious wound care is particularly vital in such injuries.

Penile fracture

This is the one injury with the most interesting accounts of mechanism of injury. Generally penile fractures occur secondary to blunt force, axial compressive forces applied to a tumescent penis.

1. Urgent repair of penile fracture is required to preserve erectile function and avoid complications
2. A circumferential degloving incision is preferred for greater visibility and access
3. If fracture involves only the Buck's fascia, the ecchymosis is limited to the penis which has the classic "eggplant" appearance.
4. If fracture involves tunica albugenia, the ecchymosis can extend along the perineal fascial planes in a "butterfly" distribution
5. Repair is done using non absorbable monofilament sutures

Patients should be informed of the risk of developing de novo penile curvature after repair

Autonomic Dysreflexia

This is a life threatening condition that occurs on the background of spinal cord injury at or above the level of T6. Early recognition and avoidance of triggers is life saving.

Basic concepts

In the neurologically intact system, any stimuli that causes sympathetic activation is dampened by the parasympathetic system, in SCI, however this sympathetic drive is unopposed. This leads to a massive sympathetic surge leading to vasoconstriction below the level of injury.

Triggers

Urological: these are the most common triggers for Autonomic dysreflexia (AD)
- Distended bladder (AUR, blocked catheter, cystoscopy)
- Bladder irritation (SPC insertion, urethral catheterisation)

Colorectal: the 2nd most common triggers for AD
- Fecal impaction
- bowel distension

Dermatological:
- Pressure sores
- skin irritation (food crumbs, abrasive clothing)
- abrasions
- fungal infections

Clinical features

- Life threatening hypertension with bradycardia
- Seizures
- Pulmonary edema
- Myocardial infarction
- Untreated may lead to death

Management of AD
Removal of the trigger is the basis of management, early recognition and prevention of AD is vital especially in the following situations:
- SCI patients
- Patients with metastatic spinal lesions(e.g. Ca Prostate)

The blocked catheter

Catheter blockage is commonplace in clinical practice.

Catheter patency is particularly important in the following cases;

1. Spinal cord injury especially those above T6
2. Obstructive uropathy in acute renal failure
3. Post prostatectomy

Generally the simplest solution to a blocked catheter is to replace the catheter. However, in some cases a few manoeuvres may be required to overcome the blockage

1. Flushing with saline using a Toomey/ bladder syringe
2. Bladder washout to evacuate clots to avert further blockage
3. Changing to a larger size, multichannel catheter
4. Bladder irrigation

Prostate exam

The prostate exam is the hallmark of urological practice. Useful information can be derived from a thorough prostate exam.

Basic anatomy

The most common method of anatomic description of the prostate is via **McNeal's Zonal anatomy**

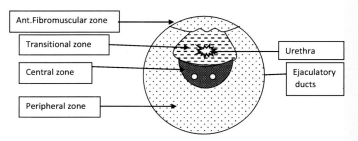

The prostate exam is part of the digital rectal exam, this should be performed routinely.

!!!Transabdominal U/S is generally not used for **routine** assessment of the prostate. Its use is commonly employed for evaluation of the kidneys and bladder in cases of bladder outlet obstruction!!!

Description of a prostate

1. Size: normal vs. enlarged(mild ,moderate and severe)
2. Symmetry: asymmetrical Vs symmetrical
3. Consistency: firm, hard, stony hard, soft, boggy
4. Surface: nodular, smooth
5. Overlying mucosa: free, adherent
6. Tenderness: none, severe, "exquisite"

Note: in trauma patients with pelvic injury a finding of a high riding prostate implies posterior urethral disruption.

Prostate massage
This is both a diagnostic and therapeutic intervention. In the diagnosis of chronic pelvic pain, chronic prostatitis and recurrent UTIs, a prostate massage as part of a "4 glass" or "2 glass" test may aide in localisation of infection site. The massage also provides symptomatic relief for patients.

Prostate biopsy

This outpatient procedure can potentially lead to life threatening complications thus strict indications must be followed.

Indications for prostate biopsy

1. Suspicious DRE
2. Raised PSA
3. Change in DRE or PSA findings in a patient on active surveillance of Ca Prostate

Prostate biopsy can be:
*   Finger guided
*   TRUS guided

The aim is to collect 10 cores from the peripheral zone (site of most cancers)

Pre biopsy preparation

1. Antibiotics- a stat dose of IV gentamycin one hour prior to procedure
2. Enema with or without rectal metronidazole
3. Post procedure short antibiotic course

These measures have been shown to decrease the occurrence of post biopsy urosepsis.

Post Biopsy Urosepsis:

A high index of suspicion is required to identify this condition early.

Urosepsis should be suspected in all patients that present with "flu-like" symptoms or other constitutional signs after a prostate biopsy.

Patients may also present with: apathy, hypothermia or lethargy.

Management:

1. Wide bore IV access
2. Fluid resuscitation
3. Broad spectrum urine- penetrating IV antibiotics (e.g. quinolones, 3rd generation cephalosporins)
4. Ensure adequate bladder drainage, catheterise if necessary

Paediatric Scrotal Swellings

Scrotal swellings

Hernias and hydroceles make up one of the commonest presentation to the OPD in children and hernia repair constitutes the largest number of operations done in most hospital settings.

Hernias: Hernias usually present with a reducible inguino- scrotal mass noted by parents when a child cries. Occasionally presents with a hard irreducible inguino-scrotal mass associated with pain, redness and vomiting in an inconsolable child that seems to have spasms of pain.

Stages of presentation:
1.   Reducible- where bowels slide in and out of the patent processus vaginalis
2.   Incarceration – when the bowel loops are trapped in the sac but viable
3.   Obstructed- as contents in the trapped bowel cause a proximal obstruction.
4.   Strangulation and gangrene – sets in if the trapped bowel has reduced blood supply and later becomes gangrenous within the hernia sac with ensuing fever and local hyperaemia and peritonitis
Premature infant (born less than 37weeks gestation)
-       More prone to incarceration and complications; must be repaired as soon as possible
Term neonates, Infants and older children
-       Can be booked more electively but parents must be counselled on the dangers of incarcerated hernia as mentioned above and the need for intervention as soon as child shows signs of incarceration(as above).

Treatment: surgical management is the mainstay of treatment, however; in experienced hands the hernia that is only incarcerated or irreducible without strangulation can be reduced by taxis and observed while awaiting definitive operative treatment.

Hydrocele: Can be confused with a hernia but is irreducible in most instances, with changes in the size being reported in the history by the parents. Infantile and childhood hydrocele is due to a *fine patent processus vaginalis* only admitting fluids. The scrotal cystic swelling of the hydrocele can will usually have a positive transillumination test and is irreducible unlike the hernia.
Treatment of a hydrocele: involves a herniotomy and drainage of the distal fluid sac via an inguinal incision

Paediatric Acute Scrotum

The Acute Scrotum

This is not an uncommon condition in the examination of an acutely ill infant or child.

Child will present with crying and pulling up of the lower limbs and at times just vague symptoms such as refusal to feed.

Torsion of testis: This is a surgical emergency. Occurs when the testis blood supply is occluded by the twisting of the testis due to a loose fixation of the testicular attachments in the scrotal tunica vaginalis. If uncorrected leads to testicular death. The left is affected more than the right.

Presentation

Neonates: rare, typically asymptomatic, can present with a hard oedematous hemi-scrotum with discoloration.

Older children:
- a history of minor trauma
- sudden onset of scrotal pain that may radiate to the lower abdomen
- general abdominal pain
- nausea and vomiting

The scrotum is exquisitely tender and the testis lies horizontal and is higher than the contralateral side and classically the elevation of the testis on the effected side does not relieve the pain as occurs with the inflammatory condition like Epidydimo-orchitis.

Treatment of torsion is scrotal exploration with bilateral orchidopexy.

Differential Diagnoses

- Torsion of the testis
- Torsion of an appendix testis
- Epidydimo-orchitis (common between birth and 6 months thereafter rare until after puberty. Common organism is E. Coli)
- Scrotal infections (e.g. neonatal staphylococcal infection)
- Infective orchitis (e.g. mumps)

Orchidopexy

Typically involves a three point fixation of testis to the Dartos fascia commonly known as the Shoemaker's method via an external Dartos pouch. The contralateral testis should be pexied routinely as it is also at risk of torsion.

AUR in Children

Not a common occurrence but may be encountered in the emergency setting.

Causes of AUR in children

Some of the causes of AUR in children are listed below:-

Congenital:

- PUV (**males only**)
- Prune Belly Syndrome
- Ureterocele (prolapsed)
- Meatal stenosis
- Urethral atresia (rare)
- Abdominal tumors (causing bladder outlet obstruction)

Acquired:

- Bladder stones
- Urethral stones
- Urethral strictures
- Bladder-bowel dysfunction
- Hinman's syndrome
- Blocked catheter in a child with an indwelling catheter

Urethral Catheterisation of a child

Inserting any tubes in the alert child can be a daunting task. Urethral catheterisation is no exception; however if done gently and swiftly can be a relatively simple procedure.

1. Choose the smallest size catheter available
2. Lubricate the urethra sufficiently to ensure smooth catheterisation
3. If using a Foley catheter, 2-3 ml should sufficiently inflate the balloon in size 6-10 catheters

Posterior Urethral Valves

PUV should be suspected in any male infant or child presenting with AUR with or without renal impairment. These children present with varying levels of complications depending on the type of urethral valves the child has.

> **Basic Concept**
>
> Posterior urethral valves represent an aberration of the embryological development of the urethra. This leads to an obstructive membrane in the posterior portion of the urethra.

Types:

Type I: two separate folds of urethral mucosa forming a one way valve extending from the verumontantum to the membranous urethra. (Most common type)

Type II: circular band of urethral mucosa extending from the verumontantum to bladder neck forming a band like constriction (these are not considered true valves)

Type III: Complete membrane in posterior urethra with a centrally located pin hole opening also known as Congenital Obstructive Posterior Membrane (COPUM)

Approach to PUV

1.   A full physical examination focused on the urological system will reveal a characteristic *"walnut bladder"*; a firm to hard distended bladder that is palpable abdominally

2.   The child may present in *urosepsis* and be acutely ill- catheter drainage of bladder, maintenance of hemodynamic and volume status are paramount in management

3.   A multidisciplinary approach with early involvement of paediatric nephrologists, and paediatric ICU care may be warranted in the face of AKI

4.   Urological intervention for definitive treatment of PUV is instituted once the child is out of immediate danger

5.   Bladder catheterisation is best done with size 5 or 6 Fr tube rather than Foleys catheters in the young infant as the balloon may obstruct the ureteric orifices in these tiny bladders.

6.   Older children can be catheterised safely with smaller sized (6, 8 or 10Fr) catheters

Note: in resource limited settings, even older children (up to pre teens) can present with PUV, these are usually incomplete valves. Despite this, these children still have chronic (usually irreversible) renal impairment

PUV ablation: This endourological procedure is carried out with a paediatric resectoscope. Various methods can be used for valve ablation however the basic principle remains;

Note: Valve children require long term nephrological follow up to monitor for the sequelae of PUV.

Phimosis & Paraphimosis

These are two very common presentations of uncircumcised young boys. Both conditions involve the prepuce; however the distinction can easy be made on clinical examination

Phimosis (non retractable prepuce) can be physiological or pathological. Physiological phimosis will resolve during toddler years (age 3) but can go up to age 5. Pathological phimosis is characterised by voiding difficulties, fibrotic prepuce with fissuring that leads to further pain when voiding. Phimosis, even when pathological, rarely requires emergency intervention.

Management of phimosis

- **Medical**: topical corticosteroids e.g. betamethasone cream twice daily for 2-3weeks
- **Surgical**: *elective circumcision*-although not an emergency, a boy that presents with phimosis with a history recurrent UTIs requires a circumcision.

Paraphimosis (non reducible prepuce) is a true urologic emergency and requires active and immediate intervention. The prepuce usually forms a constrictive ring below the glans making retraction difficult. It is further complicated by edema distal to the ring which makes reduction even more difficult.

Management of paraphimosis

- Aseptic technique
- Local or topical anaesthesia
- Manual reduction with gentle sustained pressure to oedematous prepuce while simultaneously pushing on the glans penis

---

UTIs in children

All children with UTIs should be investigated for urinary tract abnormalities, over 70% of these children are found to have a genito-urinary system anomaly which accounts for the occurrence of the UTI.

Special attention should be paid to

- Children with recurrent UTIs especially girls
- Children with a single episode of a febrile UTIs

Children with frequent episodes of diarrheal disease are prone to development of lower urinary tract stones especially bladder stones which may present as recurrent UTIs

Documentation of Important Procedures

Catheterisation

After every catheterisation it is vital to document the procedure including any difficulties faced.

Template:

Date/time

Size and type of catheter used

Amount of fluid used to inflate catheter balloon

Ease of passage of catheter (no resistance Vs resistance)

Amount and characteristic of urine drained (cloudy, concentrated, bloody, dilute)

Continuous drainage or controlled flow (flip flow valve, spigot)

Expected duration of catheterisation

Signature/ name

Example:

M/75 suspected BPH presents in AUR, catheter is inserted.

Notes:

12/12/2012, 2100hrs

Size 16 2 way Foley catheter inserted

10cc distilled water used to inflated balloon

Catheter inserted with no resistance, 600mls concentrated urine drained

Keep catheter on continuous drainage till renal function established

Dr Xyz
Unit 1 on call
> *Emergency room 4*

Cystoscopy

A common procedure in the outpatient urology setting, documentation is best represented in a **bladder diagram.**

Template:

Date/time

Type of cystoscope used

Indication for cystoscopy

Findings-

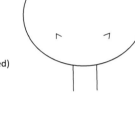

- Bladder mucosa(normal, hyperaemic, trabeculated)
- Ureteric orifices (normal, bloody efflux, not visualised)
- Lesions (size, site, consistency)
- Prostate (obstructive, bleeding, normal)
- Urethra (patent, strictured,inflamed)
- Other findings

Example:

12/12/2012, 0830hrs

Rigid cystoscopy

Indication: - Hematuria

Findings-

- *Normal bladder mucosa*
- *Ureteric orifices visualised*
- *2 x 2cm solid lesion visualised on posterior wall*
- *No other lesions visualised*
- *Prostate non obstructive*
- *Urethra patent, normal mucosa*

Dr Xyz
Unit 4
Urology unit

Supra Pubic Cystostomy

A common emergency procedure that can be done by any emergency room doctor

Template

Date/time

Closed or Open method

Size and type of catheter used

Amount of fluid used to inflate catheter balloon

Amount and characteristic of urine drained (cloudy, concentrated, bloody, dilute)

Type and size of sutures used if any

Continuous drainage or controlled flow (flip flow valve, spigot)

Expected duration of catheterisation

Signature/ name

Example

12/12/2012, 0900hrs

Closed SPC done with size 12 2 way Foley catheter

Balloon inflated with 10cc distilled water

600mls clear urine drained

Nylon 2/0 suture used to suture skin

Site dressed and catheter left on continuous drainage

Keep catheter for xy days

> *Dr Xyz*
> *Emergency room 6*
> *Unit 8 on call*

Trial Without catheter

A Trial With-Out Catheter commonly referred to as TWOC is done in the outpatient department by removing an indwelling catheter to assess patient's ability to void spontaneously.

As a general rule urethral catheters are placed for a specific purpose and for a specified duration after which they should be removed or changed as per indication.

As a guide it is worth noting the average duration of catheterisation for various catheter types and purposes.

Indication	Catheter used	Duration*
AUR in BPH	Latex uncoated	3weeks
	Latex (silicone coated)	4weeks
	Pure silicone	6-9weeks
Post prostatectomy (open)	Any type of catheter	14days
Post prostatectomy (TURP)	Any type of catheter	2days **
SPC	Latex uncoated	3weeks
	Latex (silicone coated)	4weeks
	Pure silicone	6-9weeks

*note: these are generalised guides and are subject to clinical variations and physician preference

** may also depend on surgeons preference

Dislodged Supra Pubic Catheter

A dislodged SPC is a common presentation to the emergency room. An SPC can get dislodged for various reasons:

- Attempted forceful removal by patient
- Defective valve/balloon complex
- Un-inflated or under inflated balloon on catheter insertion

Approach to the dislodged SPC

1. If a new catheter was recently inserted in an old SPC tract, simply deflate the balloon completely, gently push the catheter back and re- inflate.
2. In the case of an old catheter, completely remove and replace with a new one.

Note: A freshly inserted SPC(few hours or <7days) on SPC naïve abdomens should be handled more cautiously as the SPC tract has not yet formed and removal of catheter may lead to open cystostomy under anaesthesia

Tips:

As much as possible, always replace catheters with those of the same size. In some instances the corresponding catheter size may not be available; as a general guide the following sizes can be used for the following purposes

Indication	Catheter size(fr)
Clear urine	Adults: 14, 16,18 Children: 6,8,10(age dependent)
Infected urine(thick, Cloudy or pus)	Adults: 20,22 Children: 10,12(age dependent)
Bloody urine	Adults: 20, 22,24 (3-way)

Evaluation of LUTS

Lower Urinary Tract Symptoms (LUTS) are the most common symptom complex in urological clinical practise. The severity and combinations of this symptom complex vary from patient to patient.

Basic concepts

LUTS, though more prevalent in elderly men, are NOT peculiar to men, and are NOT synonymous with prostatic pathology; women can also have LUTS.

LUTS can generally be classified as:

Storage symptoms	Voiding symptoms
Urgency	Hesitancy
Frequency	Intermittency
Nocturia	incomplete bladder emptying
Urge incontinence	post micturition dribble

There are some useful tools that can be used in the evaluation and characterisation of LUTS;

Symptom Scores – AUA symptom score, International Prostate Symptom Score, Visual Prostate Symptom Score

Abdominal U/S- an imaging tool that can be used to assess the GU tract for causes or sequelae of LUTs

Uroflometry- characterises the nature of the urine stream and reproduces this pattern on a graphic trace. Different pathologies have distinct patterns that can be used to direct further diagnostic investigations

Cystometry- this measures the bladder pressure during filling

Pressure-flow studies (PFS) - this measures the bladder pressure in relation to the urine flow, it is done by measuring bladder pressures while patient is voiding.

Electromyography (EMG)

Uroflometry, cystometry, PFS and EMG used in combination are known as urodynamic studies- UDS

Tip: In patients with LUTS that cannot be explained or LUTS that are refractory to adequate treatment rule out a neurogenic bladder; a full neurological examination with a neurologist consult is warranted.

Urinanalysis

Urinanalysis is an informative tool in the assessment of the urological patient. It is considered an extension of the physical examination rather than an investigation and thus should be carried out routinely on all patients.

Basic concepts
Urine norms:
Specific gravity 1.003-1.030
pH5.5
No glucose or protein

Application of urinanalysis
The Mears-Stamey test also known as the four-glass test is a test to localise the site of a UTI; modifications to this test have been made and now 3 and even 2 glass tests can be used for localisation tests. Sequential urine samples are taken as illustrated below:

The Four glass test

VB1

After genital cleaning collect initial portion

VB2

The next portion is the mid stream sample

VB3

Prostatic massage is done and the secretions are collected

VB4

Post prostate massage voided sample

The test may be done with only VB2, VB3 and VB4 or alternatively VB2 and VB4. The samples are analysed individually and the sample with signs of infection (nitrites, WBC, pus cells) indicate the localisation of the infection.

VB1- urethra; VB2-bladder; VB3- prostate; VB4-prostate

Note: epithelial cells can be due to skin contamination of sample however; very high quantities could indicate malignancy and further work up e.g. urine cytology may be warranted

Further reading

➢ European Association of Urology , 2017. *EAU Guidelines 2017.*

➢ Graham Jr., S. D., 2003. *Glenn's Urologic Surgery.* 6th ed. s.l.:Lippincott Williams & Wilkins.

➢ McAnnich, J. W. & Lue, T. F., 2013. *Smith &Tanago's General Urology.* 18th ed. s.l.:The McGraw-Hill Companies.

➢ Reynard, j., Brewester, S. & Biers, S., 2013. *Oxford Handbook Of UROLOGY.* 3rd ed.

Made in United States
Orlando, FL
03 July 2025

62623008R00024